D0939901

Nanami Momozono is a high school student who was evicted from her home when her dad skipped town.
She meets the tochigami Mikage in a park, and he leaves his shrine and his kami powers to her.
Now Nanami spends her days with Tomoe and Mizuki, her shinshi, and with Onikiri and Kotetsu, the onibi-warashi spirits of the shrine.
Nanami has been slowly gaining powers as a kamisama by holding a festival at her shrine and attending the Kamuhakari, a kamisama conference in Izumo.
Nanami gets entangled in a succession fight at the tengu village on Mt. Kurama.
She ousts Yatori, an ayakashi who was sowing confusion, and releases the soul of the Sojobo from its prison, thus solving the conflict.
When Nanami returns to Mikage shrine, everything seems to be back to normal...!

Kamisama Kiss

Volume 11
CONTENTS

Chapter 61 005
Chapter 62 037
Chapter 63 067
Chapter 64 099
Chapter 65 129
Chapter 66 161
End Notes 191

Kamisama Kiss

Story & Art by

Julietta Suzuki

CHARACTERS

Mamoru
Nanami's shikigami.
Nanami Momozono
A high school student who was turned into a kamisama by the tochigami Mikage.
Tomoe
The shinshi who serves Nanami now that she's the new tochigami. Originally a wild fox ayakashi.

Kamisama Kiss
Chapter 61

CONGRATULATIONS
Hello. I'm Okazaki, Julietta Sensei's assistant. I'm here because Sensei told me "you can write something."
As I work, I look forward to what Nanami-chan and Tomoe-kun get up to every chapter. I hope the two will be together and happy soon.
My favorite character is Kayako-chan. I love her manly ways. I like Onikiri-kun and Kotetsu-kun too. My heart goes soft when they appear.
Kami-sama Kiss
Drawing them is actually pretty difficult
So I'm enjoying working on every chapter.
This was brought to you by Okazaki.

A WEDDING CEREMONY.
WHAT, WHAT? MAYBE YOU'RE GONNA DO IT TOO?
YEAH.
THE QUESTION CAME UP...
...AND I'M THINKING OF ACCEPTING IF TOMOE SAYS YES.
Yeah.

SINCE WE CAME DOWN FROM MOUNT KURAMA ...
...SOME-HOW ...
MY HEART ACHES.

WE MUST RECEIVE A NEW OFUDA.
YOU MUST GO SEE THE TOSHIGAMI-SAMA BEFORE THE NEW YEAR ARRIVES.
TOMOE-DONO.
DAMN.
BECAUSE WE'VE ALREADY LOOKED AT THE CHERRY BLOSSOMS, MY SENSE OF SEASON IS OUT OF WHACK.
IT'S STILL THE MIDDLE OF WINTER HERE.
Dash
AH.
IT'S THAT TIME OF THE YEAR ALREADY—
KKSSH
TOMOE-KUN!

WHACK
A SHINSHI WHO ASKS HIS MASTER TO MARRY HIM DESERVES TO DIE!
GET OUTSIDE!
HEH...
I DON'T KNOW WHAT YOU'RE TALKING ABOUT ...
BUT FINE, SNAKE.
I'LL SKIN YOU ALIVE AND LEAVE YOU TO SHRIVEL IN THE SUN!

STOP!
FREEZE
SO WHY AM I GETTING MARRIED?
YOU'RE NOT, NANAMI-CHAN?
NO.
I ONLY GOT A REQUEST TO DO A WEDDING CEREMONY AT THE SHRINE!
OH YEAH, FROM WHO?

Hime-miko of the Swamp
HOW CAN A CATFISH MARRY A HUMAN ?!
Y-YOU'LL NEVER KNOW UNLESS YOU TRY!
HIMEMIKO TOLD ME SHE WANTS TO GET MARRIED TO KOTARO HERE.
IT'S WONDERFUL TO BE INVOLVED IN THEIR RELATIONSHIP, FROM THEIR FIRST ENCOUNTER TO THEIR MARRIAGE CEREMONY.
EVEN IF THEY'RE JUST PLAYING HOUSE, IT'S A WEDDING CEREMONY.
HMPH
AND THEY'RE DIFFERENT SPECIES.
GRR

I'LL DO IT!
I CAN DO IT!
CUZ I'VE BEEN MATURING AS A KAMI-SAMA!
YEAH, NANAMI-CHAN WILL BE ABLE TO DO IT.
EVEN IF TOMOE-KUN DOESN'T COOPERATE, I'LL HELP YOU.
MIZUKI, THANK YOU.
HOW DARE YOU, YOU SNAKE!
OOH, BUT I FEEL BETTER NOW.
I ASSUMED NANAMI-CHAN WAS GONNA GET MARRIED AND QUIT BEING KAMISAMA.
OH?
I WON'T GET MARRIED.
NOT EVER.

TOSHI-GAMI?
YOU MUST GO TO THE TOSHIGAMI-SAMA'S SHRINE QUICK, ELSE THE GATE WILL CLOSE.
MMM.
You're right.
PLEASE GET READY.
TOMOE-DONO!
YES, THE KAMI WHO VISITS AND BRINGS CROPS FOR THE NEW YEAR.
IT USED TO BE ONE KAMI WHO WENT TO ALL THE HOMES ...
THE KAMISAMA THAT VISITS YOUR HOUSE AT NEW YEAR'S?
You offer them kagami-mochi.
...BUT HE SPRAINED HIS BACK FROM WORKING TOO HARD ...
SHRINES GO TO THE UPCOMING TOSHIGAMI'S SHRINE TO OBTAIN A NEW OFUDA EVERY YEAR.
...SO NOW TWELVE KAMI SPLIT THE WORK, ONE EACH YEAR ON A TWELVE-YEAR CYCLE.

AND SO.
WE TWO WILL GO TO THE TOSHI-GAMI'S SHRINE.
Huh?
WE TWO MEANS YOU AND ME?
CLENCH
OF COURSE.
LET US CONTINUE WHERE WE LEFT OFF WHEN NANAMI WASN'T AROUND.
JUST US SHINSHI ALONE.
...
YOU TWO ARE GOING ALONE?
WHEN ARE YOU COMING BACK?
HMM, MIZUKI MAY NOT BE ABLE TO RETURN.
Forever
NO NO, TOMOE-KUN MAY NOT BE ABLE TO RETURN ...
I-I'LL COME TOO.
NO.
IF YOU COME, SOME-THING WILL GO WRONG AGAIN.

I'M COMING TOO!
Sure!
ARGH.
SHE'S ALWAYS LIKE THIS.

SO THIS IS THE TOSHI-GAMI'S SHRINE?
IT'S THE ENTRANCE.
THERE'RE SO MANY TORII.
SO WE NEED TO PICK ONE.
SHE DOESN'T KNOW HER PLACE, AND STICKS HER HEAD INTO EVERY-THING ...
WOW.

THESE ARE THE TWELVE TORII.
GUESTS TO THE TOSHIGAMI'S SHRINE MUST PASS THROUGH HERE ...
Oh...
...AND SHOW HOW THEY'VE SPENT THEIR PAST TWELVE YEARS.
NANAMI
THAT'S MY NAME!
WHY ?!
YOU FEEL DIZZY ?!
It's like getting drunk for twelve years.
I HATE GOING THROUGH HERE ...
...CUZ MY HEAD FEELS DIZZY.
NANAMI, WAIT HERE.
THE SNAKE AND I WILL GO AND BE BACK SOON.
YOU SHOULDN'T PASS THROUGH THE TORII IN A HUMAN BODY.

IT'S ALL RIGHT!
Yeah!
SOUNDS FUN.
IT'S HAPPENING AGAIN ...
SO I GO THROUGH THE TORII WITH MY NAME ON IT.
I'M ...
...SCARED OF LOOKING BACK ON THE DAYS WHEN I SHUT MYSELF UP AFTER LOSING YONOMORI-SAMA.
She's gone
TWELVE YEARS ...
I ENVY NANAMI-CHAN, WITH HER CLEAR HEART.

NANAMI'S CAREFREE.
NOT QUITE.
SHE LIKES YOU, BUT SHE KNOWS SHE CAN'T MARRY YOU.
SHE'S SMART.
UNFORTUNATELY SHE'S NOT GOOD AT FIGURING THINGS OUT, LIKE YOU ARE.
AMAZING, TOMOE-KUN. YOU KNOW A LOT ABOUT NANAMI-CHAN.
Hmph
The air's getting stale here, so I'm going too.

...HER SWEET FRAGRANCE.
OF COURSE.
I KNOW NANAMI BEST.
HER HABITS...
...HER GESTURES...
YES.
TOMOE-KUN.
NANAMI-CHAN WENT IN FIRST, BUT SHE HASN'T COME OUT YET.

Exit
Exit
EVEN IF SOMETHING HAPPENS ...
...I'M PRE-PARED.
NANAMI
MOSTLY.
DON'T GET ANGRY.
NANAMI BEING WHO SHE IS ...
...SHE'S PROBABLY STUCK SOMEWHERE.

Hello!
I'm Julietta Suzuki.
Thank you for picking up Volume 11 of Kamisama Kiss.

I'll be happy if you enjoy reading this volume! This series runs in Hana to Yume (on sale in Japan the 5th and 20th of each month!), so I'll be happy if you read the magazines too.

Well, please come along with me!

HUH?
THAT WAS NANAMI-CHAN.
NANAMI-CHAN HAS GONE BACK TWELVE YEARS.
WHA?!
TOMOE-KUN!
Dash
Dash
Tmp
Tmp
Tmp
Tmp
THAT WAS NANAMI?
YOU'RE BACK FROM DAYCARE?
NANAMI!

WHAT IS THAT?
I got bread crusts.
I'm gonna give them to mommy.
Daddy.
LOOK.
I'LL GIVE YOU SOME-THING BETTER.
Milk
Wow.
I WON TODAY.
IT'S A PACHINKO PRIZE.
Yay! Yay!
Choco-late!

RUFFLE
SEE YOU.
TELL MOM I WON'T BE BACK CUZ I EARNED SOME MONEY.
NANAMI-CHAN.

NOW LET'S GO HOME TOGETHER. ♡
...
YOU'RE CUTE AS A LITTLE KID TOO. ★
FOUND YOU. ♡
KICK
KID-NAPPER!

DASH
DASH
DASH
WHA ...?
AH.
THAT IS NANAMI.
No mistake. Nanami's sharp.
I'VE TOLD YOU IT WAS HER!
STUPID!
I CAN'T RECOVER FROM NANAMI-CHAN KICKING ME.
YOU GO NEXT, TOMOE-KUN.
SURE.
OR THE WAY SHE DASHES AROUND.
HER RECKLESSNESS HASN'T CHANGED.
THIS NANAMI ...
...IS CUTE TOO—

IN ANY CASE, I MUST RETURN WITH NANAMI QUICK.
I'M SORRY.

DO YOU REALLY INTEND TO PAY US?
MY WIFE SAW YOUR HUSBAND AT THE PACHINKO PARLOR THIS MORNING.
IF HE'S GOT MONEY TO PLAY PACHINKO, HE SHOULD BE ABLE TO PAY HIS DEBTS!
YOUR RENT IS TWO MONTHS LATE NOW!
I'M SORRY ...

I'LL ...
...MAKE MY HUSBAND PAY BY MONDAY.
I DON'T BELIEVE THAT. YOU'VE GOT A DAUGHTER
IF YOU HAVE NO INTENTIO OF PAYIN WE HAVE TO
YOU SHOULDN'T BE RENTING WHEN YOU DON'T EVEN HAVE THE MONEY BLAH BLAH BLAH
WE'VE GOT TO MAKE A LIVING TOO BLAH BLAH

I'LL HAVE THE MONEY READY BY MONDAY.
RUB
HEY YOU GUYS, BE QUIET
BLAH BLAH BLAH YOU'LL FIND IT HARD TO LIVE HERE
I DON'T WANT TO BE SAYING THIS WHEN IT'S ONLY 50,000 YEN
RUB

NANAMI.
SMILE
WELCOME HOME.
TMP
MOMMY.

NANAMI HASN'T TOLD ME MUCH ABOUT HER PARENTS ...
...BUT I UNDER-STAND NOW.

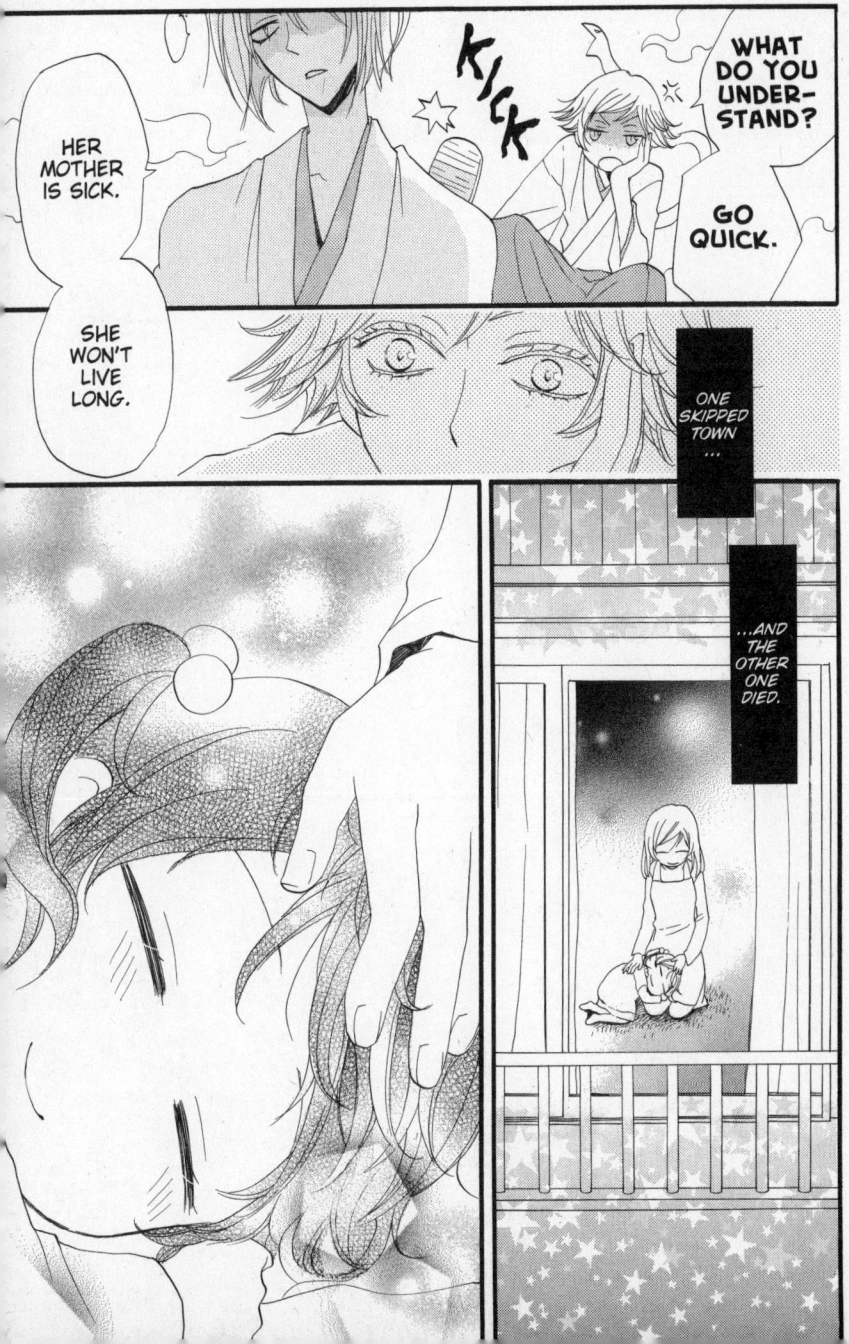
WHAT DO YOU UNDER-STAND?
KICK
GO QUICK.
HER MOTHER IS SICK.
SHE WON'T LIVE LONG.
ONE SKIPPED TOWN ...
...AND THE OTHER ONE DIED.

WAIT ...
TOMOE-KUN.
...A LITTLE LONGER.
THAT'S...
...A NANAMI I DON'T KNOW.

Kamisama Kiss
Chapter 62

THE NANAMI OF TWELVE YEARS AGO...
..LOOKS LIKE A STRANGER...

CHOMP
THIS SASA-MOCHI IS GOOD!
CHOMP
CHOMP
Ha Ha Ha!
I MADE LOTS OF IT!
I'LL PUT THE REST IN THE FRIDGE, SO... HMM?
OPEN
!! BAM
NOOO.
THE UTILITIES MONEY!
I HID IT IN THE BOTTOM OF THE FRIDGE ...

HEH HEH... I'M ALL RIGHT, I'M ALL RIGHT.
MOMMY, ARE YOU OKAY?
CLING
DAD
WOW!
I'M LUCKY.
HOW DARE YOU... YOU EVEN TOOK THIS MONEY ...
IT'S GONE!
Koff Koff
SORRY, NANAMI.
MOMMY WON'T BE ABLE TO BE WITH YOU FOREVER ...
...SO WHEN I'M GONE, DO YOUR BEST ALONE.
I WILL DO THAT ALL ALONE?
WHAT ABOUT DADDY ?
LOCKING UP, KEEPING HOUSE, EVERYTHING.

I WISH I COULD'VE GIVEN BIRTH TO YOUR SIBLINGS ...
...BUT THIS IS IN OUR BLOOD.
ALL RIGHT ?!
YEAH.
DON'T DEPEND ON HIM.
DON'T TELL HIM WHERE YOU KEEP YOUR MONEY. TELL HIM YOU DON'T HAVE ANY, EVEN IF HE CRIES AND BEGS.
WHY ?
IT HAPPENED TO YOUR GRANDMOTHER AND GREAT-GRANDMOTHER TOO.
...AND ONLY ONE DAUGHTER IS BORN EVERY GEN-ERATION.
OUR FAMILY LINE IS ALL FEMALE ...
OH.
IT'S A PRETTY ROMANTIC STORY.
BOO
I WANTED A BIG BROTHER.
SINCE THEN, ONLY ONE CUTE, HEALTHY GIRL IS BORN EACH GENERATION.
SO SEE?
ONE OF OUR ANCESTORS GOT MEDICINE FROM A KAMISAMA. IT MADE HER BEAUTIFUL WHEN SHE DRANK IT.

I WAS ABLE TO GIVE BIRTH TO A BEAUTY LIKE YOU.
Hee Hee
BUT UNFORTUNATELY, OUR FAMILY ...
WHEN GRANDMA TOLD ME, I DIDN'T BELIEVE HER AT ALL ...
...BUT NOW I'M SAYING THE SAME THING TO MY DAUGHTER!
GRAB
SO, NANAMI.
GLARE
...HAS NO LUCK WITH MEN!
WE SUFFER FROM OUR HUSBANDS!

DON'T DEPEND ON MEN.
LIVE TOUGH AND LONG BY YOURSELF.
DON'T RUIN YOURSELF LIKE MOMMY DID.
ALL RIGHT!
I SEE.
I WON'T DEPEND ON MEN!
I'LL GROW BIG BY MYSELF!
ALL RIGHT!
NANAMI'S NERVES OF IRON...

...COME FROM HER MOTHER.
SO THAT'S WHY ...
POUT
A HUMAN CHILD GROWS UP BY OBSERVING HER PARENTS.
SQUEEZE
FOR NANAMI-CHAN, HER PARENTS WERE A LIVING EXAMPLE.
SO WHY'RE YOU STAYING HERE, TOMOE-KUN?
I CAN UNDERSTAND WANTING TO WATCH CUTE LITTLE NANAMI-CHAN ...
...BUT THESE ARE ONLY NANAMI-CHAN'S MEMORIES ...
...SO THERE'S NOTHING WE CAN DO.

LET'S GET HER OUT OF THIS NIGHTMARE.
AH.
YES...
BUT...
...I ...

...WANT TO WATCH THIS NANAMI THAT I DON'T KNOW.
JUST A LITTLE MORE.
SIZZLE
JUST A LITTLE MORE ...
...

The day *Kamisama II* comes out in Japan, a book of my one-shots is coming out as well.

It's manga I sent in before I made my debut, and my debut manga is in it. Actually, the one-shots were all drawn around the time I made my debut, so you can tell I still had a lot to learn about drawing manga. I hope you'll take a look...

There're re-runs of the Moomin anime on TV nowadays, and I enjoy watching it every morning. I got the DVD boxset too! It hasn't arrived yet, but I'm looking forward to it. Moomin! Moomin! My favorite character is Moomin Mama. She soothes me.

When I said I'd like to go to Finland someday, I was told that 2013 is the year for watching the aurora borealis! So my heart is swaying. 2013! What will I be doing then?

LAST YEAR I ASKED FOR A BARBAR DOLL ...
...SO I ASKED FOR A BARBAR HOUSE THIS YEAR.
OOH.
I ASKED FOR A BICYCLE ...
...THEN MOM SAID SANTA WAS BUSY, SO I SHOULDN'T ASK FOR SOME-THING HEAVY.
WHAT ABOUT YOU, NANAMI ?
Tmp
I'M FINE.
I LOCK UP THE HOUSE EVERY NIGHT ...
...SO NO STRANGERS CAN GET IN.
1-1
NANAMI MOMOZONO
YOU GOTTA LOCK UP BEFORE YOU GO TO BED.
Silence

Nanami, you're weird.
He's not a stranger.
Santa gets in from the chimney.
CRYING IN SYMPATHY.
NANAMI-CHAN!
I CAN'T BEAR TO WATCH ANYMORE.
THIS IS LIKE A SOAP OPERA!
He likes watching TV.
SO WHO'S SANTA?
I CAN'T LET YOU HANDLE THIS.
I'LL GO NOW!
MMM.
AND YOU CAN JUST WATCH ME.

OR IT WOULD'VE BEEN DIFFICULT TO LIVE HER LIFE...
A POWERLESS CHILD WITHOUT A GUARDIAN.
NANAMI?
1-1
NANAMI MOMOZONO
NANAMI WAS FORTUNATE TO BE A HAPPY-GO-LUCKY GIRL...

NANAMI-CHAN!
MMM.
Oh no!
I'M NOT DANGER-OUS. I'M YOUR ALLY!
...
ARGH.
IT'S ME, IT'S ME. YOUR FIRST SHINSHI, MIZUKI!
It's me. I'm here for the second time.
It's been a while.
BUT YOU WOULDN'T REMEM-BER.
I REMEM-BER.

UH.
NO, I'M ...
DASH
YOU'RE THE KID-NAP-PER!
Thought so!
SLAM

Ah!
TOMOE-KUN!
Dash
Dash
Dash
GRAB
COME, THIS WAY.
LET'S GO.
Nnn?
THE KIDNAPPER IS HERE.

SERVES YOU RIGHT...
...
YEAH!
The kidnapper is here.
AARGH!
...YOU NASTY SNAKE.
TOMOE-KUN ...
I'LL KILL YOU WHEN WE GET BACK ...

TUG
YOUR EAR!
I DON'T INTEND ...
...TO FORGIVE HIM FOR SADDLING ME WITH THIS, BUT...
THEY'RE LIKE CAT EARS. YOU MUST BE ABLE TO HEAR GOOD.
It's warm.
TUG TUG
TOUCH-ING YOUR EAR IS FUN!
IT'S CUTE
...
SHEESH.
LET'S GO TOWARDS THE EXIT ...
WHAT ...
I wanna touch your ears! touch your ears!
...AM I DOING?
NNN ?

THE SCENERY IS STRANGE.
ICE CREAM
VANILLA
CHOCO-LATE
SHOJI
IT LOOKS HAZY ...
...BUT SOME PARTS ARE VERY DETAILED ...
THE DETAILED PARTS ARE THINGS SHE LOOKED AT OFTEN.
YOU WANT SOME ICE CREAM.
JOLT
I SEE...
THESE ARE NANAMI'S MEMORIES.
I...
BLUSH
I DON'T WANT ANY.

HERE.
HERE'S SOME ICE CREAM.
Th...
THANK YOU, BIG BROTHER.
Big brother
IF THERE'S ANYTHING ELSE YOU WANT, TELL ME.
I'LL TREAT YOU.
INSIDE HERE.!!

...SO MAKING YOU HAPPY IS A NO-BRAINER.
...I CAN EASILY TELL WHAT YOU WANT...
Wow.
I can eat all this?
Really?
YEAH.
Your hair's a mess.
Family Restaurant 24H
SO SMILE.
LOOK, LAID-BACK, LIKE ALWAYS ...
AND I'LL...
KIDS' Toy
Bicycles

...BE WITH YOU.
SO DON'T LOOK LIKE THAT.
THE SUN'S ...
...ABOUT TO SET.

THE SETTING SUN'S HUGE ...
WHEN THE SUN'S DOWN ...
...EVERY-ONE GOES HOME.
SCRATCH
I DON'T WANNA GO HOME.
CUZ THERE'S NO ONE THERE.
JUST ME.
I-SEE.
WHAT YOU WANT IS...
RUFFLE
Hee!

YOU'LL EVENTUALLY BECOME THE MASTER OF A LIVELY SHRINE. IT'LL BE SO LIVELY YOU'LL THINK IT'S NOISY.
YOU'RE ONLY ALONE FOR NOW.
NO.
I WON'T GET MARRIED.
HMM ?
DOES THAT MEAN I'LL GET MARRIED?
WILL I GET MARRIED AND MAKE A NEW FAMILY?
WELL, UM ...

WHY NOT?
CUZ I HAVE NO LUCK WITH MEN.
I WON'T DEPEND ON A HUSBAND.
IT'S NOT THAT YOU HAVE NO LUCK WITH MEN. YOU HAVE NO EYES FOR MEN.
SHOVE
I'LL GROW BIG MYSELF—
I'LL...
...BE ABLE TO MAKE YOU HAPPY.
I'LL GET YOU ANYTHING YOU WANT.
No one's more dependable than me
Shove Shove Shove...
I WON'T BE LURED BY FOOD AND MARRY SOMEONE I DON'T LOVE.

DO YOU ...
...REALLY, REALLY LIKE ME?
IF YOU ASK CUTELY LIKE THAT...
Shove
YEAH.

SO...
I CAN'T HELP BUT ANSWER LIKE THIS.
I LOVE YOU.

...WILL YOU MARRY ME?
HEY, NANAMI.
YOU CAN KEEP SMILING.

Sure!
I'LL BE WITH YOU...
...SO YOU CAN KEEP SMILING.

Kamisama Kiss
Chapter 63

SO WILL YOU MARRY ME?
...DID I SAY?
OOH, WHAT ...
SURE!

I WENT TOO FAR AND ASKED HER TO MARRY ME!
IF NANAMI REMEMBERS ...
WHAT DO I DO?!
...KNOWING HER ...
TOMOE, YOU ASKED ME TO MARRY YOU.
You do like me after all!
...SHE'LL CLOSE IN ON IN ME!
OOH...

HOW CAN I LIE MY WAY OUT OF IT THIS TIME...?
WHAT'S THE MATTER, TOMOE-KUN? YOU'RE FIDGETING.
SMILE
I WON'T TELL NANAMI-CHAN ...
...WHAT YOU DID TO LITTLE NANAMI-CHAN.
REALLY ?!
SO YOU DID DO SOME-THING TO HER.

STOP!
FREEZE
SHEESH... YOU TWO ALWAYS FIGHT WHEN I'M NOT WATCHING.
WHERE ARE WE? WHERE'RE THE TWELVE TORII?

WE'VE PASSED THROUGH THE TORII.
WHA?! WHEN DID I...?!
OH, SO I WAS ASLEEP.
I FEEL LIKE I WAS IN A LONG DREAM.
OH, WHAT SORT OF DREAM?
I...
...IT WAS ALL A DREAM...
...FOR HER.
AND FOR ME TOO ...
ACTUALLY ...
EVEN IF SHE REMEMBERS ...
...DON'T NEED TO DECEIVE HER...

I DON'T REMEMBER ANYTHING.
Well, who cares?
REALLY? REALLY? YOU DON'T REMEMBER THE KID-NAPPER?
KID-NAPPER? WHAT THE HECK?
YOU CALLED ME A KID-NAPPER AND KICKED ME.
WHAT?! OH NO, SORRY!
I DON'T REMEMBER ANYTHING AT ALL.
SHE...

SHE DOESN'T REMEMBER ANYTHING ?!
NOW, LET'S HURRY TO THE TOSHIGAMI'S SHRINE!
WE GOTTA HURRY, OR THE SUN WILL SET.
Hmm.
THE ENTRANCE SHOULD BE AROUND HERE.
I WONDER WHAT SORT OF KAMI THE NEXT YEAR'S TOSHI-GAMI-SAMA IS?
HEY, TOMOE.
...
TOMOE ?

YOU REALLY...
...DON'T REMEMBER?
NANAMI.
HERE.
HERE'S SOME ICE CREAM.

Ooh.
Where'd that come from?
WOW, AMAZING!
Ice Cream!
Yeah! I love it!
...
MIZUKI, YOU KNOW WHAT ICE CREAM IS?
...
Yaay!
If you like ice cream so much, I'll take you to Kotaro's work
I can? Thank you!
THEN YOU CAN HAVE IT.
Here.
He can have it, right, Tomoe?
Yummy!

The "Zakkuri Cookie Choco" (from Kabaya Shokuhin) my assistant got for me are really good, and they're my favorite nowadays.

If you find it in a supermarket, grab a box!

Nowadays, I've got three assistants working with me, so I'm able to work very efficiently. Thanks for coming.

For this volume...

...two assistants were working hard. Thank you so much.

Chomp

Chomp

WHAT'S WITH THIS DRAGON CHILD?

Grab

WHA?

JOLT

MY ICE CREAM...

A sea horse?

Looks like this...

SQUEE!
SHOVE
LET ME TOUCH YOU, LET ME TOUCH YOU!
WHAT'S A BEAST OF THE ZODIAC DOING HERE?
YOU SHOULD BE BUSY GETTING READY FOR THE NEW YEAR AT THE TOSHI-GAMI'S SHRINE.
I'M NOT A SEA HORSE!
I'M A DRAGON, NEXT YEAR'S ZODIAC!
MAYBE HE WAS CHASED OUT CUZ HE'S USELESS.
GETTING READY FOR THE NEW YEAR WOULD BE DIFFICULT WITH A CHILD LIKE THIS.
I WASN'T CHASED AWAY!
GRR

I RAN AWAY FROM HOME!
I ALSO CLOSED THE ENTRANCE TO THE SHRINE!
CLOSED THE...
THAT'S WHY WE HAVEN'T BEEN ABLE TO FIND THE ENTRANCE!
Fwip
YOU RETURN TO YOUR SHRINE RIGHT NOW AND OPEN IT!
NO.
I WON'T GO BACK TO THE TOSHIGAMI-SAMA.
THE TOSHI-GAMI-SAMA ...
...DOESN'T NEED ME ANYWAY.

THEY FEEL SO DIFFERENT.
...
THEY'RE SOFT AND FLUFFY.
RABBITS ARE CUTE.

SOB
I HATE THE TOSHI-GAMI-SAMA!
SO I'M NOT FLUFFY!

THE TOSHIGAMI REALLY SUCKS!

I'LL MAKE YOU WANT TO RETURN.
I WON'T RETURN TO THE SHRINE.
Do it, Tomoe-kun
WHAT THE HECK!

TUG
LIKE THIIIIS.
H...
HE DOESN'T LOOK LIKE THAT ...
HE MUST HAVE A WARPED PERSONALITY.
AND HE MUST LOOK LIKE THIS.
NO, HE MUST LOOK LIKE THIS.
I CAME TO GET OUR OFUDA, BUT MAYBE I WON'T BOTHER.
SOMEONE TERRIBLE LIKE HIM WON'T GIVE US OUR OFUDA ANYWAY.
THE TOSHI-GAMI-SAMA IS REALLY NICE!
HE'S HAPPY TO HAND OUT HIS OFUDA!
OH, REALLY ?

THEN I'D LIKE TO MEET ...
...YOUR KIND TOSHI-GAMI-SAMA.

HE'LL SHOW US THE WAY.
...
NANAMI-CHAN IS AMAZING.

THAT DRAGON IS STILL A KID.
AND I THINK THE TOSHI-GAMI IS WORRIED ABOUT HIM.

I'M SURPRISED YOU WERE ABLE TO CONVINCE THE DRAGON.
OH REALLY ?
HE SEEMED LIKE A PAIN TO DEAL WITH.
So stubborn

YOU WERE A CHILD YOURSELF UNTIL JUST NOW.
Smile

YOU'RE LIKE YOUR MOTHER.
YOU'RE GOOD AT TAKING CARE OF KIDS.
I'M LIKE MY MOTHER ?

Well.
MY MOM DIED WHEN I WAS SMALL ...
...SO I DON'T REMEMBER WHAT SHE LOOKED LIKE.
Smile

REALLY ?
I THINK I LOOK LIKE MY DAD.
People say a girl can be happy if she looks like her dad.
Now that you mention it...

EVERYTHING, INCLUDING PHOTOS OF HER, WERE LOST IN THE FIRE.
MOMMY.
MOMMY.
I WISH I HAD JUST ONE PHOTO OF HER.
PEOPLE CHANGE IN TWELVE YEARS.
THE LITTLE NANAMI AND THIS NANAMI ...
...ARE THE SAME, YET DIFFERENT.

SO WHERE...
SOMETHING WRONG, TOMOE?
...DID THAT LITTLE CHILD GO?

TOSHI-GAMI
HERE.
THIS IS IS THE TOSHIGAMI-SAMA'S SHRINE.
WHAAAT?!
NO WAY!
WHAT'S WITH THAT SHABBY SIGN?
THIS IS THE TOSHI-GAMI'S SHRINE!
THIS IS HIS SHRINE?!
WE CAN'T HELP IT! WE'RE BUSY!
We'll get things ready, bit by bit!
WELL WELL
LET'S GET OUR OFUDA AND LEAVE QUICKLY.
RUSTLE

POP
UH... TOSHI-GAMI-SAMA.
RYU-BO!
RUSTLE
RUSTLE
RUSTLE
TOSHI-GAMI-SAMA!
RYU-BO!

YOU FOOL!
WHERE WERE YOU?! I WAS LOOKING FOR YOU!
DON'T LEAVE ME ALONE, YOU FOOL.
SWING
I SEE.
MY THOUGHTLESS WORDS HURT HIM ...
GOOD THING YOU FOUND HIM.
I THANK YOU FOR IT.
NO PROB-LEM.
WE JUST RAN INTO HIM ON HIS WAY HOME.

THE PREVIOUS DRAGON TOSHIGAMI RETIRED, AND I TOOK OVER ...
...BUT THIS IS THE FIRST TIME I'LL BE THE REIGNING TOSHIGAMI ...
...AND I'M WORRIED ABOUT WHETHER I CAN FULFILL MY DUTIES.
I'VE GOT NO TIME TO RENOVATE THE SHRINE.
CRUMBLING
I'M AFRAID I'M NOT UP TO IT...
I WAS CHOSEN AS THE NEW DRAGON TOSHIGAMI ...
...YET MY ANIMAL RAN AWAY ...
SHEESH
THE NEW YEAR WILL BE AN UNLUCKY YEAR FOR ALL HUMANS, SO THERE!
Sorry!
WHAAAAA!
IT'S NOT EVEN NEW YEAR'S YET!

YOUR DRAGON ...
...LOVES YOU.
TH...
THINGS ARE FINE, TOSHIGAMI-SAMA.
A TOSHI-GAMI-SAMA WHO'S SO LOVED BY HIS ANIMAL ...
...MUST BE REALLY DEPENDABLE.
PLEASE TAKE GOOD CARE OF THE NEW YEAR.

DO I...
...MISS HER ...
...A LITTLE?
LET ME GIVE YOU MY OFUDA FOR THE NEXT YEAR.
AND THIS IS A TOKEN OF MY GRATITUDE.
THANK YOU, TOCHI-GAMI.
THE CHILD OF TWELVE YEARS AGO IS NO LONGER HERE.

YOU MENTIONED YOU DIDN'T HAVE A SINGLE PHOTO LEFT ...
...SO THIS IS WHAT I SAW IN YOUR TWELVE TORII.
SOME-THING WRONG, NANAMI?

MOM.

THEY DON'T DISAPPEAR.
I SEE.
THAT LITTLE CHILD. HER MOTHER.
THE FEELINGS THAT WERE THERE ...

...WILL REMAIN WITHIN NANAMI FOREVER...
...EVEN IF SHE DOESN'T REMEMBER.
I THINK I LOOK LIKE MY MOM!
Won't I?
WHEN I GROW UP, I'LL BE A BEAUTY LIKE HER.
I DON'T REALLY WANT TO DO THAT.
...TO KEEP BEING MY MASTER FOREVER!
I WANT NANAMI-CHAN ...
NOT TO WORRY.
THAT WORRIES ME.
I HOPE YOU DON'T GO OFF AND GET MARRIED LIKE YOUR MOM.
You're good at taking care of children too.

I WON'T GET MARRIED.
PROBABLY.
Probably won't?!
HMPH.

THEY CAME TO RECEIVE THE TOSHIGAMI-SAMA'S OFUDA, AND SAW THIS.
NO NEED TO SAY HELLO
TAKE AS MANY AS YOU WANT.
I FEAR FOR THE COMING YEAR...

WELL!
WE COVERED NANAMI-CHAN'S PARENTS, THE TENGU-KUN ARC IS FINISHED...
SO NEXT IS MY TURN!
HMPH.
You fool
KICK
AM I THE ONLY CHARACTER WHO'S SERIOUS ENOUGH TO WANT TO MOVE THE MAIN STORY FORWARD?!
WHO IS THAT?
UH, HE APPEARED IN VOLUME 7.
HIS STORY.

Chapter 64
I WANNA SEE A "SEA OF FIRE."
YOU KNOW THAT PHRASE "SEA OF FIRE"?
THAT MEANS THE FLAMES ARE LIKE AN OCEAN.
FOR INSTANCE, IF WE BURN THIS PLACE ALL THE WAY TO THE EDGE OF THE SKIES AND THE EARTH ...
CRACKLE
CRACKLE
CRACKLE
...WILL IT TURN INTO A SEA OF FLAMES?
SIZZLE
DON'T.
FSSH

YOU CAN BURN THINGS, BUT YOU CANNOT PUT THE FLAME OUT.
DO NOT PLAY WITH FIRE WHEN YOU CANNOT CONTROL IT, AKURA-OH.
IF YOU WANT A SEA OF FLAMES ...
...I'LL SHOW YOU AN OCEAN OF KITSUNEBI THAT DEVOURS THE CRIMSON FIRE...
...SOME-DAY.

Kamisama Kiss
Chapter 64

KIRI-HITO.
ARE YOU AWAKE ?
HOW'RE YOU FEELING? MAY I COME IN?
YOU HAVEN'T EATEN ANY-THING TODAY.
YOU MUST EAT SOME-THING—
SUT

GOOD.
YOU LOOK FINE TODAY.
I MADE YOUR FAVORITE—STIR-FRIED LIVER AND CHINESE CHIVES.
A BOY MUST EAT A LOT TO GET HEALTHY.
OR YOU WON'T GET BETTER.
...
ALL RIGHT?
Stroke
Oh!
YOUR HAND IS COLD.
ARE YOU KEEPING YOUR ROOM WARM?
It's going to be cold today.
GRAB

I TOLD YOU I'M BUSY.

YOU DON'T NEED TO PREPARE FOOD FOR ME.

DON'T CARE FOR ME ...

...MOTHER.

A-ALL RIGHT.

I'M SORRY I INTER-RUPTED YOUR STUDIES.

HOW-EVER.

FOOD IS A DIFFERENT MATTER!

HERE

EAT IT ALL.

PUT THE DISHES OUTSIDE YOUR ROOM WHEN YOU'RE DONE.

I FIND IT DIFFICULT DEALING WITH THAT WOMAN.
Tch
OHO, THIS IS BEEF LIVER, KIRIHITO-SAMA!
LIVER AND CHINESE CHIVES!
THE GATE TO YOMOTSU-HIRASAKA WAS SEALED, BUT THERE'RE OTHER WAYS TO GET THERE.
THIS IS A STONE MIRROR I MADE USING SOIL I BROUGHT BACK FROM THE LAND OF THE DEAD ...
WHEN THE FREQUENCY IS RIGHT, IT SHOULD BECOME AN OPENING TO THE LAND OF THE DEAD.
AND THE DOOR WILL OPEN SOON...

I'LL GO TO THE LAND OF THE DEAD AGAIN ...
...AND THIS TIME I'LL BRING BACK MY BODY.
YOU TWO STAY HERE.
SHIKIGAMI AND YOKAI TURN TO DUST WHEN THEY COME IN CONTACT WITH THE AIR DOWN THERE.
BUT... KIRIHITO-SAMA, WILL YOU BE OKAY ALL ALONE?!
YEAH.
THIS IS THAT WOMAN'S HAIR.
AS LONG AS I HAVE THIS ...
ARE YOU GOING, KIRIHITO-DONO?
STEP
HOW GALLANT YOU ARE!

This is delicious!
CHOMP
CHOMP
I WOULD LOVE ...
...TO ACCOMPANY YOU TO THE LAND OF THE DEAD.
WHAT'RE YOU HERE FOR?!
OOPS!
YOU'RE THAT RUDE FELLOW WHO VISITED A WHILE AGO!
SERVES YOU RIGHT.
I WAS CAUGHT OFF GUARD.
WELL...I DISGRACED MYSELF WITH THAT KURAMA BUSINESS.

YOU MADE ALL THOSE PROMISES, YET YOU DARED TO RETURN HERE EMPTY-HANDED ...
...YATORI.
...YOU REMEMBER MY NAME?
SO ...
Tears
KIRIHITO-SAMA.
GRR
DO I LOOK STUPID ENOUGH TO FORGET ...
...SOME-ONE'S NAME?
OF COURSE I DO.
WHAP
Kirihito-dono...

THE STONE MIRROR IS OPENING!
THE DOOR TO THE LAND OF THE DEAD...
...IS FINALLY OPENING.
Kirihito-dono! I would like to accompany you.
NO! NO!
NO PROB-LEM.
WHA ?!
COME IF YOU WANT TO.
IF YOU CAN KEEP UP WITH ME.
IT'S BEEN SEVERAL MONTHS ...

...SINCE I LAST WENT UNDER-GROUND TO THIS WORLD OF STENCH AND IMPURITIES.
I...
THOSE WHO CANNOT BEAR THE POISONOUS AIR RETURN TO DUST.
MY BODY IS LYING...
...SOME-WHERE IN HERE.
...WILL GET MY BODY BACK!

HOW BIG ...
SO THIS IS THE LAND OF THE DEAD ...
WELL WELL
SO WHERE DID KIRIHITO-DONO FALL?
I DIDN'T THINK IT WOULD BE SO HOT ...
AH.
KIRIHITO-DONO.

HUH ?
I'M SURPRISED YOU'RE STILL ALIVE.
I'M GLAD. I WAS WORRIED ABOUT GETTING LOST ...
A HALF-YOKAI TURNS TO DUST WHEN THEY COME IN CONTACT WITH THE AIR HERE.
I THOUGHT YOU'D TURN TO DUST LIKE TETSU-KIMARU ...
WHAT ARE YOU?
WHY DO YOU INVOLVE YOURSELF WITH AKURA-OH?
...
I...
Umm...

IT IS TRUE.
DO NOT LIE. I DON'T ...
...know you
I DON'T REMEMBER HIM ...
GRR GRR
I USED TO SERVE AKURA-OH-SAMA IN THE PAST.
Well.
Slap Slap
I WAS SHY AND WAS ALWAYS CHIRPING IN A CORNER.
AKURA-OH-SAMA WOULDN'T REMEMBER ME, THOUGH.
HIS ONLY ALLEGIANCE WAS TO HIS DESIRES AND HE DID NOT CARE FOR OTHERS.
WELL, TO PUT IT MILDLY, HE WAS PURE EVIL.
...SO YOU WOULDN'T KNOW ABOUT AKURA-OH-SAMA.
KIRIHITO-DONO SEEMS YOUNG ...

SWEAT SWEAT
ARE YOU LISTENING, KIRIHITO-DONO?
BUT AKURA-OH-SAMA ...
IT'S HOT DOWN HERE ...
...KEPT ONE FOX YOKAI BESIDE HIM.
BUT THERE WERE MANY WHO WANTED TO FOLLOW HIM, EVEN IF AKURA-OH-SAMA DID NOT CARE ABOUT THEM...
...AND I WAS ONE OF THEM.
HOW-EVER.
ONE DAY AKURA-OH-SAMA AND THE FOX-DONO PARTED WAYS.
NO AYAKASHI COULD WIN AGAINST THOSE TWO ...
...AND EVEN THE KAMI UP IN THE SKIES COULDN'T DO ANYTHING ABOUT THEM.

THINGS WENT DOWNHILL FROM THERE.
THE FOX-DONO DIS-APPEARED ...
...AND AKURA-OH-SAMA'S BODY WAS SENT TO THE LAND OF THE DEAD.
GRAB
DO YOU KNOW WHY THEY PARTED WAYS?
IT'S BECAUSE THE FOX BECAME SPINELESS.

THAT FOX BASTARD FELL IN LOVE WITH A HUMAN GIRL...
...AND WANTED TO BECOME HUMAN HIMSELF.

Today I shall make hamburger steaks, which Nanami loves.
STIR STIR
Mmm!

Assistant

Okazaki's Kamisama Working Hell

Recipe ①

In volume 11, I am introducing recipes of dishes that Juli Sensei liked. I made them while everyone was working.

◎Pork wrapped with plums and shiso leaves

①Salt and pepper the pork loin.

②Remove the pits from the pickled plums, and smash them using the side of the cooking knife.

③Remove the stem of the shiso leaves, and chop them up.

④Layer a shiso leaf and some plum on the pork, and roll it up.

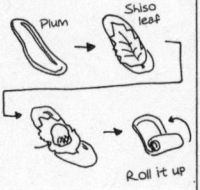

To be continued.

IT'LL BE NEW YEAR'S IN THREE DAYS!
So hurry, hurry.
...
Wah!
Wah, Nanami-chan!
BAM
YOU HAVEN'T FINISHED CLEANING THE WAREHOUSE!
YOU'RE GOOFING OFF AGAIN.
MMM, HAMBURGER STEAKS.
LOOKING FORWARD TO IT.
...
Toss
Toss

I SEE.
FLAP FLAP
THE FOX-DONO WAS PRETTY UNMANLY ...
...AFTER ALL.
IT'S HOT DOWN HERE!
WHERE ARE WE?
IT FEELS LIKE WE'VE WALKED QUITE A BIT ...
...BUT IS AKURA-OH-SAMA'S BODY STILL FAR AWAY?
IT FEELS LIKE IT HAS GOTTEN EVEN HOTTER ...
...DOESN'T IT, KIRI-HITO-DONO?
FOUND IT ...
I'VE FOUND MY BODY...
I NEVER THOUGHT IT WOULD BE ABANDONED IN A PLACE LIKE THIS ...

WHA?
I'M SURE OF IT.
MY BODY IS ON THE TOP OF THAT BURNING MOUN-TAIN.
WHAT IS THAT MOUNTAIN OF FLAMES ?!
THE KAMI ARE BURNING WHAT THEY CANNOT DEAL WITH THEMSELVES ...
THAT PLACE IS THE GARBAGE DUMP OF THE LAND OF THE DEAD.

HOWEVER...
KIRIHITO-DONO ?!
...EVEN THOSE FLAMES CANNOT TURN MY BODY TO ASHES.
MY BODY REGENERATES ...
SOME-THING WRONG, KIRIHITO-DONO?
...AND KEEPS GETTING BURNED...
...FOR ETERNITY.
NOW THAT WE KNOW WHAT HAS HAPPENED, LET US RETURN FOR NOW.
KIRIHITO-DONO.
THAT'S WHAT'S HAPPENING TO MY BODY...
IF WE STAY HERE, YOU'LL SHRIVEL UP.

HOW DARE YOU! MY BODY'S RIGHT IN FRONT OF ME...
BUT WE ARE NOT IMMORTAL ...
...SO WE CANNOT CLIMB THAT MOUNTAIN ...
...UNLESS ...
...THERE IS A WAY TO PUT OUT THOSE FLAMES.

DAMN.
DAMN!
IT'S HIS FAULT I'M LIKE THIS NOW...
...AND I TRULY CURSE HIM FOR IT...
...YET I CANNOT GET MY BODY BACK WITHOUT HIS HELP...
FASH

SIGH ...
CLACK
WE HAVE RETURNED.
KIRIHITO-SAMA!
WAKE UP, KIRIHITO-SAMA!
WHAT HAVE YOU DONE TO KIRIHITO-SAMA ?!
COME ON. I HAVEN'T ...

...
HEH HEH.
WITHOUT HIS "HELP."
I WAS AWFULLY TIMID.
I'LL USE WHAT I CAN.
I DON'T CARE ABOUT ANYTHING ELSE IF I CAN GET MY BODY BACK.
YES.

KNOOK
KIRI-HITO-SAMA!
BLACK SMOKE IS COMING OUT OF THE STONE MIRROR!
...IS LEAKING FROM THE STONE MIRROR ?!
THE POISON OF THE LAND OF THE DEAD...
SHIIT
MON-JIRO!
KIRI-HITO-SAMA.
WE MUST SEAL THAT OPENING.
NO.
WE CAN'T SEAL THE OPENING UNLESS WE BREAK THE STONE MIRROR.

TO DO THAT...
I CAN'T AFFORD TO SEAL IT.
...I CAN STAND TO HAVE THIS RESIDENCE FILL WITH POISON.
I NEED TO GET BACK MY BODY FROM THE LAND OF THE DEAD.
I CAN LIVE WITH THAT.
KIRIHITO.

...
KIRI-HITO.
HOW'RE YOU DOING WITH YOUR STUDIES?
SUT
I GOT SOME SWEET PEACHES, SO I BROUGHT THEM FOR YOUR EVENING SNACK ...
I TOLD YOU I'M BUSY ...
...MOTHER ...

Kamisama Kiss
Chapter 65

MONJIRO...
MONJIRO...

WHAM
TAKE THESE BAGS TOO.
SURE.
WAIT, WAIT.
Hey!
THIS IS THE FIRST NEW YEAR'S EVE I'VE SPENT AS KAMISAMA.
SIGH.
I THREW OUT THE LAST OF THIS YEAR'S TRASH.
MANY THINGS...
...HAPPENED THIS YEAR ...

Safe birth
Love
Good Grades
Good business
Traffic safety
I STAYED UP ALL NIGHT TO MAKE OFUDA FOR NEW YEAR'S.
...BUT I FEEL ...
OUR SHRINE DOESN'T SELL GOOD-LUCK CHARMS OR HAVE PAPER FORTUNES ...
...SO I DECIDED TO GIVE OUT THESE OFUDA TO WOR-SHIPPERS WHO COME FOR NEW YEAR'S.
...LIKE I'M DOING A LITTLE BETTER AS KAMI-SAMA.
LET ME SEE.
SHP
I HOPE THEY'RE ENOUGH.
I MADE TWENTY-FIVE OF THEM.
TRAFFIC SAFETY. GOOD BUSINESS. WARD OFF EVIL.
NANAMI-CHAN, YOU'RE SO CONSIDER-ATE.

NOOO!
CRUSH
WHAT'RE YOU DOING?! I DID MY BEST!
YOU SHOULD FEEL SORRY FOR THE WORSHIPPERS, WHO'LL BE FORCED TO TAKE HOME THOSE POORLY-WRITTEN OFUDA. AND YOUR HANDS SMELL OF TANGERINES...
DO YOU INTEND TO GIVE OUT THOSE SHABBY OFUDA?!
!!

BUT.
I WANT TO HAND OUT SOME OFUDA FOR NEW YEAR'S.
DON'T WORRY.
MIKAGE'S WOODEN OFUDA SHOULD STILL BE IN THE WAREHOUSE.
THOSE WILL BE ENOUGH.
WOODEN OFUDA.
YOU MEAN THE ONES THAT WERE TOSSED IN A BOX?
THEY WEREN'T TOSSED, THEY WERE PUT AWAY.
UH...
OUR WOR-SHIPPERS WILL BE HAPPY TO RECEIVE MIKAGE'S WOODEN OFUDA.
Unlike yours.
OH NO.
SOME-THING WRONG?

I THREW THEM ...
GLOOM
...IN THE TRASH.
IN THE TR...
Wah
THEY LOOKED OLD AND USELESS.
I...
I'M SORRY.
DON'T SCOLD ME—
I SEE.
SIGH
TOO BAD YOU THREW THEM AWAY ...

I'M A BIT EMBARRASSED...
...THAT I THOUGHT...
...I WAS DOING A LITTLE BETTER AS KAMISAMA.
safety
good
good
MY TSURIKI SHOULD BE STRONGER NOW ...
BUT EVEN IF I CONGRATULATE MYSELF ...
NOW SHE REALIZES
OF COURSE, THIS ISN'T THE SCHOOL CULTURE FESTIVAL...
THESE ALL LOOK TOO HANDMADE...

...IT'S NO USE IF TOMOE HAS THAT LOOK ON HIS FACE.
SHUT
CREAK
HE'S GOING OUT.
WHERE'S HE GOING AT THIS TIME OF NIGHT?
IT'S TOMOE.

TOMOE.
OH? I THOUGHT HE WENT IN HERE.
IS HE...
...LOOKING FOR THE REST OF THE WOODEN OFUDA?
IT'S DARK.
I NEED SOME LIGHT.
THUD
HUH?
DASH
DASH
AND I HEAR SOMETHING...
THE AIR SUDDENLY FEELS DIFFERENT ...

A FOOT!
GYAH!
GRAB
SHEESH.
WHAT THE HELL ARE YOU DOING HERE?!

WAH!
TOMOE, FOUND YOU!
"FOUND YOU" ?!
DON'T FOLLOW ME WITHOUT PERMISSION!
YOU WERE ABOUT TO GET CRUSHED.
BY THAT FOOT
WH-WHERE AM I?
WHAT WAS THAT FOOT ?
It's dark.
THIS IS THE MIDDLE OF THE OTHER WORLD.
AND YOU WERE WALKING BEYOND THAT WHITE LINE ...
POINT
THE MAIN ROAD OF THIS OTHER WORLD.
THE MAIN ROAD?

AH, THE ROAD BETWEEN OUR WORLD AND THIS WORLD.
IT'S NOT A REGULAR ROAD.
IT'S A ROAD WHERE LARGE NON-HUMAN BEINGS WALK.
A SMALL BEING LIKE YOU WOULD BE KNOCKED OVER!
THE ROAD IS ESPECIALLY CROWDED AT THE END OF THE YEAR.
YOU REALLY DON'T KNOW YOUR PLACE.
GLOOM
YOU STICK YOUR HEAD INTO EVERY-THING ...
WELL SINCE YOU'RE HERE, I CAN'T DO ANYTHING ABOUT IT...
...BUT DON'T FOLLOW ME AGAIN WITHOUT PERMIS-SION.
GLOOM
IF YOU WANT TO FOLLOW ME, TELL ME...
...AND THEN I'LL CHOOSE A SAFE WAY.
GLOOOOOM
UNTIL THIS MORNING ...

SO.
WHERE'RE YOU GOING?
SHOPPING.
...I THOUGHT I WAS DOING BETTER AS KAMI-SAMA...
SHOPPING? WHERE?
YOU CAN SEE IT NOW.
IT'S THE AYAKASHI MARKET HELD AT THE END OF THE YEAR.
THE HIDDEN MARKET.

THERE ARE SO MANY YOKAI.
WOW, I'VE NEVER COME TO AN AYAKASHI MARKET.
YOKAI'S SAKE
IT'S HELD AT THE END OF EVERY YEAR.
A HUMAN KAMI IS RARE AMONG ALL THESE YOKAI.
STAY WITH ME IF YOU DON'T WANT TO BE SOLD AT A SHOP.
...
WHERE'RE YOUR SHOES?
I'M NOT WEARING ANY.
WHY NOT?
CUZ I DIDN'T THINK I'D END UP HERE.
UH.
YOU'RE WEARING YOUR PAJAMAS ?!
YES! PA-JAMAS! I COULDN'T HELP IT!

TCH.
HERE.
WEAR MY ZORI.
NO! YOUR ZORI ARE BIG AND HARD TO WALK IN.
Toss
WEAR THEM ANYWAY.
I'LL BE EMBARRASSED AS SHINSHI ...
...IF MY MASTER WALKS AROUND BAREFOOT.

Assistant

Okazaki's Kamisama Working Hell

Recipe ②

⑥ Coat the pork with flour.

⑦ Heat up a frying pan, put a little oil in it, and cook the pork.

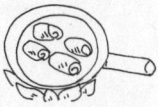

⑧ Pour a little soy sauce for flavor, and it's done.

Stir-fry some veggies as garnishing and it's done!

You can use kidney beans stir-fried in butter instead of the pickled plums and beefsteak leaves.

Try it!

I CAME AFTER TOMOE, DRESSED LIKE THIS.

I CAUSED TROUBLE FOR TOMOE AGAIN.

SOMETHING WRONG, NANAMI?

MOREOVER...

I SUCK AS KAMI-SAMA...

I GOTTA DO A BETTER JOB.

I DON'T WANT TOMOE...

HURRY.

...ANY MORE THAN HE IS NOW.

...TO BE DISAPPOINTED IN ME...

Wood
HMM.
THIS IS PRETTY GOOD.
20 silver
YOU'RE RIGHT!
IT SMELLS SWEET.
I CAN MAKE THIRTY OFUDA WITH THIS.

YOU KNOW THE GOOD TREES, MASTER.
THIS IS THE BEST TREE WE HAVE.
I'LL TAKE THIS.

How much money is 20 silver?
ARE YOU SURE?
ISN'T IT EXPENSIVE?
IT'S ALL RIGHT.

WE'LL MAKE WOODEN OFUDA WITH THIS TOKU-TOKU WOOD.
20 silver
IT'S A GOOD AROMATIC TREE, AND HELPS WARD OFF EVIL.

MIKAGE SHRINE IS CELEBRATING NEW YEAR'S FOR THE FIRST TIME IN TWENTY YEARS.
...THAT HE'S PRETTY SERIOUS ABOUT HIS DUTIES.
WHA!
So gimme a dis-count.
AFTER SPENDING ALMOST A YEAR WITH TOMOE, I'VE REALIZED...
AND THAT FOR TOMOE...
THAT HE REALLY CARES ABOUT THE SHRINE.

...I'M THE KAMISAMA OF THAT PRECIOUS SHRINE.
LOOK, TOMOE.
IT'S A KIMONO CLOTH WITH STARS ON IT.
IT'S POPULAR WITH YOUNG GIRLS.
I'D BUY IT IF I WERE A HUNDRED YEARS YOUNGER.
I CAN SEE WHY. IT'S SO CUTE.
HEY.
LET'S GO.
WAIT WAIT!
HOW DO I LOOK?
IT'S NOT FOR YOU.

WELL, LEAVING ME ASIDE ...
...HOW ABOUT WE WRAP THE WOODEN OFUDA IN CUTE CLOTH.
NO. YOU ALWAYS WANT TO DO SOMETHING UNNECESSARY.
TOMOE-SAMA?
AH, YOU CAME TO SHOP TOO?
YES.
THIS IS OUR LAST SHOPPING TRIP FOR THIS YEAR.
IT'S TANUKO ...
...FROM THE BROTHEL!
IS IT REALLY YOU? ★
TOMOE-SAMA.

WE'RE THE MOST JUNIOR EMPLOYEES, SO WE CAN ONLY SHOP AFTER OUR SENIORS HAVE FINISHED.
SO THE CUTE HAIRPINS ARE ALMOST ALL SOLD OUT.
IF I KNEW I WAS GOING TO RUN INTO YOU, I'D HAVE WORN MY FAVORITE HAIRPIN.
UGH.
AND, I'M WEARING MY PAJAMAS ...
TOSOU
...WHEN I BUMP INTO THE ENTER-TAINMENT PROS!
THE HAIRPIN LOOKS LOVELY ON YOU.
NOT AT ALL.
Truly.

OH.
WHO IS THAT?
...NO-BODY.
SHE'S JUST WITH ME.
I'VE STILL GOT SOME WORK LEFT. I MUST RETURN NOW.
DO COME SEE ME NEXT YEAR! ♡
SURE.
...
"NO-BODY" ...
WAH!
FALL
TRIP

WHY DID YOU FALL? YOU ALL RIGHT?
I'M ALL RIGHT ...
SO I'M NOT A KAMISAMA.

SO TOMOE WENT OFF ALONE ...
SIT HERE QUIETLY ...
...AND COVER YOUR HEAD WITH THIS.
I REALLY SUCK TODAY ...
OUCH ...
...
I'M NOT TOMOE'S KAMI-SAMA...
Fortune
...YOUNG MISS?
ARE YOU LOST ...
YOUNG MISS.

OH REALLY ?
YOU WANT AN ANSWER.
BUT I CAN SEE YOU'VE LOST YOUR WAY.
NO.
WH-WHAT DO YOU MEAN BY "AN ANSWER"?
SO YOU DO WANT TO KNOW.
No, that's not what I meant.
SKOOCH SKOOCH
THEN DRAW ONE.
Fortunes
THIS FORTUNE LOTTERY WILL ANSWER YOUR QUESTION.
AND IT ONLY COSTS THREE SILVER!

THAT'S WHAT I'D LIKE TO SAY!
LEAVING.
BUT YOU CAN DRAW ONCE IF YOU'LL GIVE ME THAT UMBRELLA.
THIS ?
ASK WHAT YOU WANT TO KNOW, AND DRAW ONCE.
THE FORTUNE YOU DRAW ...
...WILL ANSWER YOUR QUESTION.
WHAT...

STRIPES AND CHECKS.
NOT QUITE.
THEY DON'T SUIT NANAMI.
DON'T YOU HAVE ANY OTHER ZORI?
YOUNG GIRLS LIKE THESE.
NO WAY.
MASTER IS A PICKY FOX.
I'M IN A HURRY. SHOW ME SOME-THING ELSE.
WELL UM.
WHAT SORT OF ZORI WOULD LOOK GOOD ON YOUR MISS?
...DOES TOMOE...
...THINK OF ME?

...
FLOWERS.

FLOWERS THAT ARE ...
...PURE ...
...LOVELY ...
...AND DIGNIFIED.

A BUD...
I'LL TAKE YOUR UMBRELLA, YOUNG MISS ...
...TAKE CARE ...
I'VE GOT A LONG WAY TO GO ...
...BUT ...
...HE DOES EXPECT A LITTLE OF ME ...
I HOPE A DAY COMES...
...WHEN THIS BUD WILL BLOOM.

Kamisama Kiss
Chapter 66

I FEEL STRANGE.
BY PUTTING THIS FLOWER IN MY HAIR ...
SIT HERE QUIETLY ...
...AND COVER YOUR HEAD WITH THIS.
...I CAN HEAR TOMOE SPEAK SOFTLY.

IT'S A HUMAN.
WE'VE FOUND ANOTHER HUMAN.
WE'RE LUCKY TODAY.

THEY'RE YOKAI!
!
GOOD. LET'S COOK THEM TOGETHER IN ZOUNI SOUP.
SHE'S WANDERED IN FROM THE HUMAN WORLD!
HOW DARE YOU COOK ME IN ZOUNI SOUP!
WHO DO YOU THINK I AM?!
...A HUMAN CHILD?!
IS THAT...

I WON'T LET YOU KIDNAPPERS GET AWAY WITH IT.
LEAVE THAT CHILD HERE, AND GO AWAY.
I'M NANAMI MOMOZONO, A TOCHIGAMI!
Ahhh!
SHALL I FOLD HER UP AND CARRY HER?
Sweets
I FEEL UNEASY FOR SOME REASON.
FOOD AND DRINKS
SOME-THING'S WRONG ...

AND, I MADE HER CARRY A LEAF THAT WARDS OFF EVIL.
IF SHE COVERS HER HEAD WITH IT, EVIL AYAKASHI WON'T BE ABLE TO SEE HER.
See you, Tomoe!
TOMOE'S VIEW
I LEFT NANAMI IN A PLACE WHERE AYA-KASHI WON'T SEE HER...
CALM DOWN, TOMOE.
WHAT DO YOU NEED TO WORRY ABOUT?
I'VE BECOME AWFULLY TIMID...

WHERE'S THE STUPID WOMAN WHO HAD THAT UMBRELLA?
SHE RAN OFF.
YOU SEEM TO BE LOOKING FOR SOME-THING.
MISTER FOX.
...AND SHE WENT TOWARD THE MAIN ROAD.
TWO YOKAI WERE CHASING HER ...
AND SHE'S STRONGER THAN YOU THINK.
NO NEED TO GO. THAT YOUNG MISS IS A TOCHIGAMI.
OF COURSE I AM!
YOU'RE GOING TO RESCUE HER.
I'VE BEEN IN THIS BUSINESS FOR MANY YEARS ...
I CAN TELL.
YOU'RE JUST A FORTUNE-TELLER. WHAT DO YOU KNOW?!

SO I CAN SEE THE TRUE QUALITY OF THINGS.
I'LL TELL YOUR FORTUNE. IT'S ONLY THREE SILVER...
I WILL NOT LISTEN TO A FORTUNE-TELLER'S BABBLE.
I'M RIGHT.
SHE'S A GIRL WHO COMES TO THIS WORLD BAREFOOT IN HER PAJAMAS.
SHE NEEDS ME. OTHERWISE SHE CAN'T DO ANYTHING.
IF I DON'T FIND HER QUICK, IT WILL BE TOO LATE!

TCH. WHERE'S SHE HIDING?
SHE RUNS FASTER THAN A KID.
SHE MUST BE AROUND HERE. LOOK FOR HER. LOOK FOR HER.
PANT
PANT
I CAN'T KEEP RUNNING AWAY.
THEY NABBED A KID.
I CAN'T FIGHT!
OH NO!
I CAN'T USE THEM!
Traffic safety
Safe birth
Good business
Ward off
BUT NONE OF THEM ARE BLANK!
RUSTLE
THERE'RE WHITE OFUDA IN MY POCKET!

...
SOB ...
TOMOE!
I'LL BREAK YOUR NECK IF YOU DON'T KEEP QUIET.
TCH, THE BRAT'S AWAKE.
MOMMY!
THE WHITE LINE...
...I SEE IT OVER THERE...

I WALKED THAT ROAD WITH TOMOE.
IT'S A ROAD WHERE LARGE NON-HUMANS WALK AROUND.
A SMALL BEING LIKE YOU WOULD BE KNOCKED OVER!
THAT MEANS.
POP
HE WHO RUNS AFTER TWO HARES WILL CATCH NEITHER!
BAM
THERE'S A REAL TREAT IN FRONT OF YOU ...
...YET YOU BOTHER DEALING WITH THAT KID?

...YOU'LL LIVE A THOUSAND YEARS LONGER.
IF YOU EAT ME, A TOCHI-GAMI ...
A THOUSAND YEARS!
LEAVE THE KID BEHIND.
CAP-TURE THAT WOMAN!
CATCH ME IF YOU WANNA LIVE LONG.
DASH
HEY ...
...WAIT!
ALL RIGHT!

LET GREED BLIND YOU, AND COME AFTER ME!
IF I CAN ONLY REACH THAT MAIN ROAD!
AND IF...
...MY OFUDA WORKS!

STOMP

STOMP
BOOM

PANT
PANT
STOMP
STOMP
STOMP
STOMP
...
I'M ALIVE ...
STOMP
STOMP
GAH ...
HOW DARE YOU BRING US HERE...?
STOMP
I WISH YOU'D GOTTEN STEPPED ON, TOO.
STOMP
STOMP
STOMP
TOO BAD.
I'M FINE.

As long as I have this ofuda on me ...
I TOLD YOU, I'M A TOCHI-GAMI.
Traffic safety
...my safety here is guaran-teed.

NO WAY.
I'LL GET YOU EVENTUALLY, TOCHIGAMI.
GAH ...
AH.
TOMOE.

FWOOSH
AHHH!
DID YOU SEE ME, TOMOE ?!
MY OFUDA REALLY WORKED—

OOPS, WE HAVE TO TAKE THAT KID BACK TO THE HUMAN WORLD.
Or, she'll be kidnapped by another yokai.

I THOUGHT I WAS GONNA GET EATEN.
Mommy!
Ah-ha-ha
SHE ISN'T HUMAN.
But I'm glad.
OF COURSE SHE'S NOT. HUMANS DON'T WANDER IN HERE SO EASILY.

Waah!
I WAS SCARED.

DON'T GET CAUGHT AGAIN.
NOW ...
...GO BACK TO YOUR MOTHER.
I WILL.
...
WHAT IS IT, TOMOE ?
NOTHING.
Bad-mouthing me again ...
SHE'S A FLOWER ...

Thank you for reading this far!

This time, I had Okazaki-san, who's done a great job assisting me since Odette, draw a guest manuscript and some sidebars. Thank you!

I write a blog, and I twitter as well.

My blog

http://suzujujugem.jp/

I write about my work and my daily life, so please come take a look.

If you have any comments, please let me hear you.

Julietta Suzuki
c/o Shojo Beat
VIZ Media, LLC
P.O. Box 77010
San Francisco
CA 94107

Thank you.

BECAUSE YOU WENT WANDERING OFF, NOW IT'S THE LAST DAY OF THE YEAR.

A MAGNIFICENT LILY. A GOLDBAND LILY.

SO WHAT WERE YOU DOING?

OOPS.

He forgot her zori.

Woo, what cute chrysanthemums.

MANY MANY THINGS HAP-PENED THIS YEAR.
SO.
I TOLD YOU NO WORK UNTIL THE 20TH!
MR. TASAKI, REFUSE THOSE JOBS.
I'M GONNA CONCENTRATE ON WRITING SONGS FOR NOW.
HUH ?
I DON'T WANT ANY OTOSHI-DAMA ...
BOOM
?!
ZAT
WELL WELL.

SHINJURO-SAMA!
THIS DOOR IS FLIMSY.
M...MY BROTH-ERS.
IT HAS BEEN A WHILE!
AND BOTAN-MARU.
SO.
WHAT BUSINESS BRINGS YOU HERE, MY BROTH-ERS?
SOJOBO SENT US HERE.
AS YOUR ELDERS, WE CAME TO CONFIRM WHETHER YOU'VE BEEN TRAINING THIS YEAR...
WHAAAN
...WITHOUT LOSING YOURSELF IN THE HUMAN WORLD.

WELL THAT'S WHAT JIRO'S SAYING ...
...BUT AS WE WERE FORTUNATE ENOUGH TO MEET OUR YOUNGER BROTHER AGAIN ...
...WE, AS THE REPRE-SENTATIVES OF MOUNT KURAMA, CAME TO SEE HOW YOU'RE DOING.
AND WE'D ALSO LIKE YOU TO TAKE US TO THE TOCHIGAMI'S SHRINE, SINCE WE OWE HER SO MUCH.
THAT'S WHY BROTHER JIRO TAGGED ALONG ...
THE OLD YEAR IS ENDING...

...AND A NEW YEAR IS COMING FOR EVERY-ONE.
Fidget
Fidget
LISTEN, KOTARO.
WHY DON'T WE GO TO MIKAGE SHRINE FOR NEW YEAR'S?
IT'S THE SHRINE MS. MOMOZONO WORKS AT. ISN'T IT A BIT FAR?
KA-SHAK
KA-SHAK
I WANT TO GO WITH YOU, KOTA.
AND I'LL CHECK OUT THINGS FOR OUR WEDDING CERE-MONY...
AH.
LOOK, HIMEMIKO. I'VE BROKEN MY RECORD!
...
KOTA!
NEXT YEAR. NEXT YEAR FOR SURE.

You should've resigned yourself by now.
Hime-miko-sama.
Oh, my Himemiko-sama is very passionate.
PLEDGE YOUR LOVE TO ME!
Wah!
IT WAS A BUSY YEAR. I CRIED AND LAUGHED UNTIL THE VERY THE END...

DID YOU MAKE ANOTHER HAORI FOR ME?
NO, THIS IS A FURISODE.
A FURI-SODE?

YOU'RE TOO OLD TO WEAR ONE!
Ha Ha Ha!
Crackle
I think

...BUT IT WAS A REALLY GOOD YEAR.
IT'S DONE! ♡

THIS FURISODE IS FOR THE TOCHIGAMI.
I SPENT SEVEN DAYS MAKING IT, A THANK-YOU GIFT FOR HER SAVING YOU.
YOU WILL DELIVER IT, WON'T YOU?
I WILL.
MY EN-COUNTERS WITH SO MANY PEOPLE ARE MY TREASURES.
THEY'LL BECOME NOURISH-MENT FOR THE COMING YEAR.
WOW, LOOK AT THIS!

The female kami aims for world peace with her tsuriki.
I'M SO PROUD OF HER.
WOW.
MONTHLY LIVING KAMI? THERE'S A MAGAZINE FOR EVERYTHING.
20 MOST POPULAR LIVING KAMI
30,000 VOTES TOTAL!
NO. 1
KAYAKO HIRA
NO. 2
EDOMON
KAYAKO IS RANKED NUMBER ONE IN THIS YEAR'S LIVING KAMI POLL!
NANAMI-CHAN, WHY DON'T YOU PARTICIPATE?
OOH, I WANNA BE PROUD OF YOU TOO.
YOU CAN, YOU KNOW.
NAH.

Yes.
OF COURSE.
YOU CAN PARTICIPATE BOLDLY.
REALLY ?!
TOMOE-DONO, THE LIVING KAMI AREN'T RANKED IN ORDER OF APPEAR-ANCE.
Monthly Living Kami
I THINK YOU'LL BARELY MAKE IT TO NUMBER EIGHTEEN.
B...
BUT YOU ...
YUP.
Monthly Living Kami
...DO THINK OF ME AS A FLOWER THAT WILL BLOOM SOMEDAY.

TOMOE-KUN, WHEN WERE YOU HONEST ENOUGH TO TELL HER THAT?
I HOPE ...
HOLD IT.
WHO THE HELL ...?
BONG
BONG
Ah! THE NEW YEAR'S EVE BELLS ARE RINGING!
HAPPY NEW YEAR!
WHA ?
...WE CAN SPEND MANY YEARS WELCOMING THE NEW YEAR TOGETHER.

The Otherworld

Ayakashi **is an archaic term for yokai.**

Kami **are Shinto deities or spirits. The word can be used for a range of creatures, from nature spirits to strong and dangerous gods.**

Onibi-warashi **are like will-o'-the-wisps.**

Shikigami **are spirits that are summoned and employed by** ***onmyoji*** **(Yin-Yang sorcerers).**

Shinshi **are birds, beasts, insects or fish that have a special relationship with a kami.**

Tengu **are a type of yokai. They are sometimes associated with excess pride.**

Tochigami **(or** ***jinushigami*****) are deities of a specific area of land.**

Honorifics

-chan **is a diminutive most often used with babies, children or teenage girls.**

-dono **roughly means "my lord," although not in the aristocratic sense.**

-san **is a standard honorific similar to Mr., Mrs., Miss, or Ms.**

-sama **is used with people of much higher rank.**

Notes

Page 14, panel 4: Kagamimochi
Rice cakes piled one on top of another in order of size. *Kagamimochi* literally means "mirror rice cake" and are used as a New Year's offering for the toshigami, then cut and eaten on January 11.

Page 17, panel 3: Torii
***Torii* is a Shinto archway or gate.**

Page 26, panel 2: Bread crusts
Japanese bakeries often sell bags of crusts cut from bread loaves for a small price.

Page 26, panel 5: Pachinko
Pachinko is a gambling game often described as a cross between pinball and slot machines. Players earn winnings in the form of pachinko balls, which can be traded in for prizes. Winnings can also be surreptitiously exchanged for cash.

Page 39, panel 2: Sasamochi
***Mochi* (sticky rice cakes) wrapped in *sasa* (bamboo leaves).**

Page 77, panel 3: Seahorse
Seahorses are called *tatsunoko* in Japanese, which literally means "dragon child."

Page 78, panel 3: Beast of the Zodiac
The Japanese zodiac is very similar to the Chinese one, except the pig is a boar.

Page 87, panel 3: Ryu-bo
***Ryu* literally means "dragon," and *–bo* is an honorific for boys.**

Page 144, panel 2: Zori
Japanese sandals, worn with kimonos.

Page 164, panel 2: Zouni soup
A soup with rice cakes, veggies, and other ingredients eaten at New Year's.

Page 182, panel 3: Otoshidama
***Otoshidama* are gifts of money given to children by adults on New Year's Day in little envelopes of Japanese paper.**

Page 186, panel 3: Haori, furisode
A *haori* is a lightweight silk jacket that is worn over a kimono. It is traditionally a part of a man's formal outfit. A *furisode* is a kind of kimono for young, unmarried women characterized by long sleeves.

Page 190, panel 2: New Year's Eve bells
One hundred eight bells rung by Buddhist temples at New Year's. The number is commonly described as the number of earthly desires humans possess.

Julietta Suzuki's debut manga *Hoshi ni Naru Hi* (The Day One Becomes a Star) appeared in the 2004 *Hana to Yume Plus*. Her other books include *Akuma to Dolce* (The Devil and Sweets) and *Karakuri Odette*. Born in December in Fukuoka Prefecture, she enjoys having movies play in the background while she works on her manga.

KAMISAMA KISS
VOL. 11
Shojo Beat Edition

STORY AND ART BY
Julietta Suzuki

English Translation & Adaptation/Tomo Kimura
Touch-up Art & Lettering/Joanna Estep
Design/Yukiko Whitley
Editor/Pancha Diaz

KAMISAMA HAJIMEMASHITA by Julietta Suzuki
© Julietta Suzuki 2012
All rights reserved.
First published in Japan in 2012 by HAKUSENSHA, Inc., Tokyo.
English language translation rights arranged with
HAKUSENSHA, Inc., Tokyo.

The stories, characters and incidents mentioned
in this publication are entirely fictional.

No portion of this book may be reproduced or transmitted
in any form or by any means without written permission
from the copyright holders.

Printed in Canada

Published by VIZ Media, LLC
P.O. Box 77010
San Francisco, CA 94107

10 9 8 7 6 5 4 3
First printing, November 2012
Third printing, June 2015

www.viz.com www.shojobeat.com

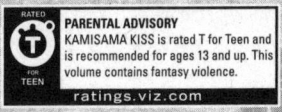

A **Publisher's Weekly** bestseller!

What happens when the hottest boy in school
...is a girl?!?

Find out in these 3-in-1
collections of the hit shojo series!

Hana-Kimi

Story & Art by HISAYA NAKAJO

Mizuki Ashiya has such a crush on a track star named Izumi Sano that she moves from the U.S. to Japan to enroll in the all-male high school he goes to! Pretending to be a boy, Mizuki becomes Sano's roommate...

...but how can she keep such a big secret when she's so close to the guy she wants?

IN STORES NOW!

3-in-1 Vol. 1 ISBN: 978-1-4215-4224-9
3-in-1 Vol. 2 ISBN: 978-1-4215-4225-6
3-in-1 Vol. 3 ISBN: 978-1-4215-4229-4

Only **$14.99 US / $16.99 CAN** each!

Hanazakari no Kimitachi he
© Hisaya Nakajo 1996/HAKUSENSHA, Inc.

www.viz.com

You've read the manga, now see the power of a kiss in action!

Kamisama Kiss

FROM THE DIRECTOR OF FRUITS BASKET

BUY IT TODAY!

Get exclusive collectibles in the Goddess Edition including:

- A replica of Nanami's hair stick
- A Tomoe lucky amulet
- A folding fan, tote bag, art postcards and more!

YOU SHOULD BE WATCHING
FUNIMATION.COM/KAMISAMA-KISS

© JS/H·K All Rights Reserved. Licensed to FUN. Produced by TMS. TMS FUNIMATION

Natsume's BOOK of FRIENDS

STORY and ART by
Yuki Midorikawa

Make Some Unusual New Friends

The power to see hidden spirits has always felt like a curse to troubled high schooler Takashi Natsume. But he's about to discover he inherited a lot more than just the Sight from his mysterious grandmother!

$9.99 USA / $12.99 CAN *
ISBN: 978-1-4215-3243-1

On sale at **store.viz.com**
Also available at your local bookstore or comic store

www.shojobeat.com

Natsume Yujincho © Yuki Midorikawa 2005/HAKUSENSHA, Inc.
* Price subject to change

ratings.viz.com

www.viz.com

Can love trump a cursed life?

Sawako's a shy, lonely, pure-hearted student who just happens to look like the scary girl in a famous horror movie! But when she manages to befriend the most popular boy in school, will her frightful reputation scare off her best chance for love?

kimi ni todoke

From Me to You

By Karuho Shiina

Find out in the *Kimi ni Todoke* manga—
BUY YOURS TODAY!

Winner of the 2008 Kodansha Manga Award
(shojo category)

On sale at **www.shojobeat.com**
Also available at your local bookstore or comic store

www.viz.com

KIMI NI TODOKE © 2005 Karuho Shiina/SHUEISHA Inc.

This is the last page.

In keeping with the original Japanese comic format, this book reads from right to left—so action, sound effects, and word balloons are completely reversed. This preserves the orientation of the original artwork—plus, it's fun! Check out the diagram shown here to get the hang of things, and then turn to the other side of the book to get started!